SCOTLAND

THE

NATURE

OF·THE

LAND

PHOTOGRAPHS·OF·NATIONAL
NATURE·RESERVES·IN·SCOTLAND

COLIN BAXTER

First published in Great Britain in 1987 by
Colin Baxter Photography Ltd
Lamington, Biggar, Lanarkshire, ML12 6HW
and
The Nature Conservancy Council
Joint copyright © Colin Baxter Photography Ltd
and The Nature Conservancy Council, 1987, 1988
Photographs © Colin Baxter

Reprinted 1988

British Library Cataloguing in Publication Data

Baxter, Colin
    Scotland: the nature of the land:
    Photographs of national nature reserves
    in Scotland
    1. Nature areas – Scotland – Pictorial
    works
    I. Title
    639.9'.09411   QH77.G7

ISBN 0-948661-00-3

Text and Editing
Alan Edwards, Edinburgh

Cover and Design
Charles Miller Graphics, Edinburgh

Printed by
Frank Peters Printers Ltd., Kendal

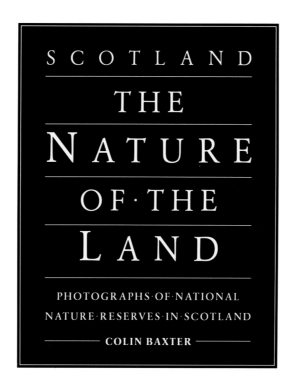

SCOTLAND
THE
NATURE
OF · THE
LAND

PHOTOGRAPHS · OF · NATIONAL
NATURE · RESERVES · IN · SCOTLAND

COLIN BAXTER

NATURE
CONSERVANCY
COUNCIL

PUBLISHED IN EUROPEAN YEAR OF THE ENVIRONMENT 1987-88

CONTENTS

BIOGRAPHICAL NOTES

Colin Baxter was born in 1954. He studied photography in Edinburgh from 1978-81, and now lives in rural Lanarkshire. His work has become well-known through postcards, books and exhibitions. Previous books are 'Scotland – The Light and the Land' (1985), 'Colin Baxter's Edinburgh' (1986), and 'The Lakes' (1987).

Christopher Smout is head of the Department of Scottish History and Chairman of the Committee for Economic and Social History at the University of St Andrews. He is also a member of the Royal Commission on Ancient and Historical Monuments of Scotland and of the Committee for Scotland, Nature Conservancy Council.

front cover Inverpolly   **back cover** Hermaness   **opposite** Glen Tanar

THE NATURE OF THE LAND

Scotland's National Nature Reserves are one of the wonders of the European Environment. To visit St Kilda, or to stay on Rhum, are among the experiences of a lifetime. To walk through the oakwoods of Ardnamurchan on a spring morning, or among the ancient pines of Rothiemurchus when they are lit with the flames of autumn birches, is to feel the spirit lifted by the perfection of the place. Colin Baxter has wonderfully captured the wildness, the sense of peace, the feeling of belonging to a greater, natural world which we all experience amid such beauty. Yet the Nature Conservancy Council is not charged by its governing statutes to preserve the National Nature Reserves because of these qualities, but because of their outstanding scientific interest. That feature may or may not be obvious to the casual eye: the gannets of Hermaness command the attention; the liverworts of Beinn Eighe are more elusive, but not less important in their significance to Scotland's nature. The natural fabric is a heritage preserved by the Nature Conservancy Council for all of us: it is very precious, very fragile, and a great responsibility to hand on intact to the next generation.

Fully to understand the National Nature Reserves, the nature of the land in which we live, we have to see them not as fragments of a pristine wilderness untouched by the hand of man, but as products of ten thousand years of interaction between man and nature. Therein lies part of their importance. The reserves are both survivors and records of this interaction, which began in the Mesolithic Age and was already old when the Roman legions occupied the southern half of Scotland nearly two thousand years ago. The first human settlers, typified by those whose sites have been excavated near Morton Lochs in Fife, were hunters. Neolithic man brought agriculture, and the nibbling of his sheep and cattle, accompanied by the use of fire to keep open the pastures from encroaching trees, began the long period of reducing the cover of the natural woodland that has continued to this day. In all this the hand of man was assisted by thorough-going alterations in the climate. It became windier and wetter, so that pine, birch and oak had a diminishing chance of re-establishing themselves as the peat cover grew thicker in the north and west. Then man produced the first cereals and in the Iron Age introduced the plough. By the time the Romans came it is altogether possible that population was quite dense, and that a great deal of corn was grown to feed the legions. We should not believe the old image of a Scotland still covered with one great wood, the 'Caledonian Forest', where the Picts lay in ambush for an encumbered army. Certainly there were wide tracts of woodland, especially in the Highlands, with wolves and wild cattle, but even this is likely to have been open, relatively sparse cover, rather than a matter of dense canopies.

This landscape is most clearly seen today in the National Nature Reserves of the Spey valley and Deeside, in ancient pine woods like Abernethy, Glen Tanar and Rothiemurchus, where stands of Scots pine up to two hundred years old alternate with heather, bog, bilberry and birch scrub. Such a wood may advance and retreat with the varying pressures of grazing and burning. It was not, in historic times, very much damaged by felling, though timber might be removed from it from time to time, sometimes on a quite intensive scale. This was because any forester before the present century would remove only the best trees (unless, of course, he was under instructions to clear fell and re-use the land for agriculture, which was unusual). In doing so, he would incidentally break open the cover of peat and heather, and seeds from the cones of younger trees left behind would readily germinate, occasionally assisted by planting from a nursery of native Scots pine. Natural regeneration came about much more easily in the eastern and central Highlands than in the west, where the peat was thicker and climate less favourable, but generally all that an attentive proprietor needed to do was to set a dyke round the wood, to keep out grazing animals, and nature would do the rest.

These open pine woods, with trees of varying ages and heights, their open spaces and undrained pools, are a refuge for many insects and several species of bird, such as Scottish crossbills and crested tits, that cannot be found elsewhere. Hardly less interesting are the surviving woods of relict birch, of which those at Creag Meagaidh are a splendid example – in May they become a lacework of pale green leaves, white stems, and singing willow warblers and redstarts. Both are the complete antithesis of commercial forestry's stands of manicured Sitka and Lodgepole, planted to throw nothing but darkness and sterility over the woodland floor. Few claims are more ignorant or insulting than those which maintain that planting in this manner is restoring Scotland's 'natural' cover.

In the west, the main component of semi-natural woodland is not pine or birch but sessile oak, clothing the sea-lochs of Argyll and Inverness, the shores of Loch Lomond and the banks of the Trossachs. In spring, when the buds open, the ground is dappled with bluebell, primrose, wood anemone and many species of fern; it is almost as beautiful in the russets of autumn. The older trees and many rocks are thickly encrusted with lichens, which may take decades to establish: a 'hoary oak' of ancient lore was one so grown with lichen that it resembled a greybeard man. Most lichens are highly sensitive to air pollution and no longer survive on trees round the main cities or in the south-east of Britain. These thick and wonderful growths are a scientific guarantee to the beholder that the air of the West of Scotland is still as pure as it feels in the lungs.

The history of these beautiful western woods has been much misunderstood, Scottish Lowlanders and English ironmasters being readily blamed for their destruction and diminution. The truth is almost exactly the opposite. There is no evidence that for hundreds of years before the eighteenth century they covered any greater area than they did when the ironmasters finally withdrew. Many reports in that century suggest that they were under threat from the uncontrolled grazing of the Highlanders' beasts, for whom woods were pasture and winter shelter rather than a source of timber. The outsider came and gave them greater value as woods: indeed, the Commissioners of Forefeited Estates after the Jacobite rebellions were so concerned to preserve and extend them that they issued their agents with bushels of acorns to plant where they thought fit. The woods were valuable as a source of charcoal for the iron furnaces at Bonawe, Invergarry and elsewhere, and, even more importantly, as a source of bark for the tanneries of the south of Scotland and Ireland. They were treated as coppice and felled in rotation: but felling an oak tree, or any other deciduous tree, will not kill it, as felling would kill a pine. From the stool a new oak will grow in due course, providing it is preserved from the tooth of goat, sheep, cow and deer. Often the regrown tree will be double or triple-trunked and many of the oaks in the western woods today show signs of that earlier cutting. All the woodland owner had to do was to maintain the fences and keep out the peasants' animals and the oaks took care of themselves. National Nature Reserves like Taynish wood and Ariundle in Argyll are preserved today for the importance of their flora, animal and insect life. That they are so beautiful is a bonus; and they stand as a monument of industrial archaeology to those misrepresented iron-masters and tanners who, by exploiting them, kept them alive for us.

In fact, even industrial man in earlier centuries was a better custodian of our woods than farmers and foresters of our own generation. The last thirty years have seen an unparalleled destruction of natural woodland by grubbing up, grazing, neglecting and replanting with alien conifers. No amount of schemes for new planting, even of broadleaf woodlands, can make up for the destruction of those traditional woods. There is simply no way to recreate their wonderful interlocking systems of trees, flowers, insects, mosses, lichens and birds, even in hundreds of years.

As with the woodlands, so with the moorlands, True, the high tops of Cairngorm are a land where man is still dwarfed by nature; the biggest area of true wilderness in Britain, a place of eagles, Arctic flora, unmelting snow patches and rock still bare from the Ice Age. But elsewhere what we see is not untouched and pristine, but land modified by centuries of pressure from grazing and burning. Remains of farming settlements from the Iron Age to the pre-clearance house are common on the moors, which are a treasure house of early archaeology. Sheep bite more closely than cattle, and the shift in emphasis of Highland farming towards sheep in the nineteenth century modified the flora in its own way. Deer graze differently again and when, after about 1880, sheep farming became less profitable than the maintenance of ground as sporting estates for deer and grouse, the numbers of deer quickly increased. They may be more numerous today than at any time in the past, as a result of man's economic and social choices.

Particularly precious in the scientific sense are those moorland areas where habitat has remained relatively less modified by grazing. At Ben Lawers in Perthshire one can see very clearly how different the flora is on rocks and ledges the sheep could not reach. The mountain harbours many limestone-loving flowers in such small refuges. Even more important examples are the great mosses and peatbogs of the far north, areas so wild and so wet that the density of animals could never be very great, though they contain many traces of early human settlement in the drier places. A significant pro-portion of all Europe's surviving blanket mire is found in the flow country of the north and its rare breeding birds are famous. This is one area under very heavy threat from forestry interests who, in this bleak country, grow tax advantages for the wealthy investor but no trees that would ever be regarded as economically viable except in the fairy-tale world of subsidy. A small proportion of the area is pro-tected as Sites of Special Scientific Interest and one, limited, National Nature Reserve is here, Blar nam Faoileag. Their preservation is important but will do little to limit the irreversible damage afforestation is likely to inflict on the remainder of the area. Its destruction, for such pathetic gain, is a poor way to mark the European Year of the Environment.

Along the spectacular coasts of Scotland, man's pressures are everywhere evident. I am glad I played as a child along a tideline that was still free of plastic detritus and oil. Such conditions will never now return, even to the remotest shores, for man's filth has become ubiquitous. On the other hand, man's treatment of the sea and its resources has by no means all been nature's loss. A hundred years ago the elegant fulmar was restricted to one breeding colony on St Kilda: now it is found on all the National Nature Reserves that have cliffs, from Hermaness to the Isle of May and on countless less restricted sites around the Scottish coast. The reason is thought to be the amount of fish offal made available when modern trawling began late in the Victorian period. The seabirds of Scotland are an important international resource and the greatest colony of all, St Kilda, has been recognised as a site of global importance to conservation. A number of species such as the gannet and the puffin have been increasing in recent decades in many colonies because of the protection afforded them at the nesting site. But some alteration in fishing practices, such as large-scale harvesting of the sand eel population to provide a fishmeal for growing more surplus grain in Europe, could send the numbers plummeting again.

Estuaries, with their seething flocks of wildfowl and waders, their distinctive flora and their marine worms and crustaceans, need to be protected from indiscriminate reclamation. The National Nature Reserves at Caerlaverock on the Solway and Nigg Bay in Cromarty are memorable places to visit on a winter evening when the grey geese and the wigeon flight over the saltings. The machair on the Hebrides, with its carpet of flowers nurtured by shell sand over the peat and its shallow lime-rich lakes full of rare pond plants, is an unusual habitat by international standards. A reserve like Loch Druidibeg on South Uist ensures that some, at least, will be saved from reseeding and draining programmes designed by the European Community to grow still more unwanted food. Regulations from the sixteenth and seventeenth centuries forbidding the pulling of bents and the destruction of whins on the dunes are among the earliest Scottish conservation laws, passed to prevent erosion of such fragile pastures.

We live now, as we have always lived, in a very delicate balance with nature. Our National Nature Reserves are a monument to this balance and a reminder that, although we have much more power now to upset and alter that balance with nature, when we erase all trace of what is beautiful, varied and interesting we destroy a heritage and create a monotony for all time. We can restore a medieval castle, after a fashion, but there is no such thing as a restored forest or a rebuilt estuary. An ancient meadow can be wiped out in an hour, but well-intentioned resowing with wild flower seeds will not bring back its original communities of flowers, mosses, butterflies and beetles in the lifetime of any one of us. The fabric of nature is literally irrepaceable.

The National Nature Reserves are preserved for the nation in perpetuity, yet they represent only the tip of the iceberg as far as the Nature Conservancy Council is concerned. There is also the selection of Sites of Special Scientific Interest to consider. These are chosen to represent the finest habitats in each area and to preserve them (under the Wildlife and Countryside Act of 1981) from basic change, without altering the basis of ownership. Some of these will indeed be local nature reserves, or belong to voluntary bodies such as the Royal Society for the Protection of Birds or the Scottish Wildlife Trust. Most remain, and are likely to remain, in the hands of local landowners. The Council works hard too, through its local officers, advising farming interests, commenting on land-use plans, and liaising with voluntary bodies to help select local wildlife sites. These sites have no statutory protection, but they form a third rank of interesting and accessible places which can be enjoyed by everyone.

Education is the key to the long-term conservation of Scotland's heritage. Fifty years ago, when we knew little and cared less for most of our historic buildings, it was common enough practice to rip down an ancient castle or a medieval tenement, or to deface a Georgian mansion if it got in the way of 'development'. Many a small burgh and not a few large towns damaged their economic prospects for all time by making themselves so ugly that no-one would want to live in them or visit them once the short-term boom of this or that economic activity had passed. So it is today with the countryside. We must hope the time will come when it will be as unthinkable to destroy an ancient wood, or drain a thousand-year-old moss as it would be to pull down a pre-Reformation kirk or bulldoze Skara Brae. That beauty begets jobs and improves the quality of life, because people want to live in and visit beautiful places, is a lesson the town planners learnt with painful difficulty. Our countryside is under such a threat that we need to learn that nature conservation also pays, in every sense; and we need to learn quickly, or most of what is finest will be taken from us.

Meanwhile, we have Scotland's magnificent National Nature Reserves, our own nature reserves, to enjoy with pride. Let us ensure that they do not become isolated spots of beauty and ecological interest in a defaced land, but rather the centrepiece of Scotland's national effort to keep the nature of the whole land beautiful.

– T C Smout

THE NORTH WEST

Scotland's north west is unique in both a British and a European context and it is appropriate that the region should have a large and representative selection of reserves. Although sparsely populated, particularly in parts of Sutherland and Wester Ross, crofting and fishing still exert a major influence on the daily life of the communities here; but in ecological terms the most significant impact on this great area of moor and mountain has been the retreat of the ancient pine forests. In reserves such as Beinn Eighe fragments of that original forest are being conserved and extended, while elsewhere, at Strathfarrar for instance, regeneration projects are underway. Many native forest species are thus being encouraged to re-colonise the region. To the geologist and botanist the north west is of considerable interest. Knockan Cliff at Inverpolly and Glen Roy are internationally famous geological sites, as is Inchnadamph, which is also of botanical importance. The western islands too have many unique features; the machair of South Uist, the great variety of habitats found on Rhum, and St Kilda's spectacular seabird colonies, among them.

opposite Water-lilies at Loch Druidibeg, South Uist

ST KILDA

St Kilda has been included in the World Heritage List as the first nomination from Scotland, an accolade this far-flung group of islands richly deserves. Lying well to the west of Harris in the Outer Hebrides, St Kilda has the most spectacular cliff scenery to be found anywhere in the British Isles. It can boast both the highest sea cliffs and rock stacks in the land, and Hirta, the main island, is the most remote inhabited place in British waters. The small deserted village there is gradually being restored by the National Trust for Scotland, to whom the islands were bequeathed in 1957. Above all St Kilda is renowned as the breeding ground for vast numbers of seabirds: it has the biggest gannetry in the world, a large colony of puffin, and the oldest and largest colony of fulmar in the British Isles. All around the cliffs the sky is filled with a swirling cloud of birds, their cries carrying far out to sea. A number of rare species, including Leach's petrel and Manx shearwater, are found here and great skuas, a comparatively recent arrival, now nest on the island grasslands. Between 1930 and 1957 St Kilda was uninhabited and, as a legacy from that period, flocks of feral Soay sheep roam over the islands of Soay and Hirta.

above Boreray at dawn *opposite* Cleits in Village Bay, these small dry-stone structures were used for drying peat and storing food

14 The world's largest gannetry, Stac an Armin with Boreray behind and Stac Lee to the right

Soay and the north west cliffs of Hirta, Soay Stac and Stac Biorach separate the islands

16   Stac an Armin seen through a natural arch in Glen Bay, Hirta

left Mist rising over Boreray's western cliffs *right* looking down from Mullach Bi on Hirta

18 Boreray's massive rock stacks, Stac an Armin and Stac Lee, are the highest in Britain at 191 metres and 165 metres respectively

'The Gap' on Hirta with Oiseval rising beyond, the island grasslands are fertilised by seabirds and enriched by the sea-spray

St Kilda's main island, Hirta, rises smoothly and steeply from Village Bay (opposite) to the hill of Conachair which falls away in a 430 metre precipice (above left), making it the highest cliff in British waters. Like Rubha Mhuirich (above right) it is a major breeding site for seabirds. At one time two to three million pairs of puffin nested on the islands, most notably on Dun, but their numbers have declined in recent years.

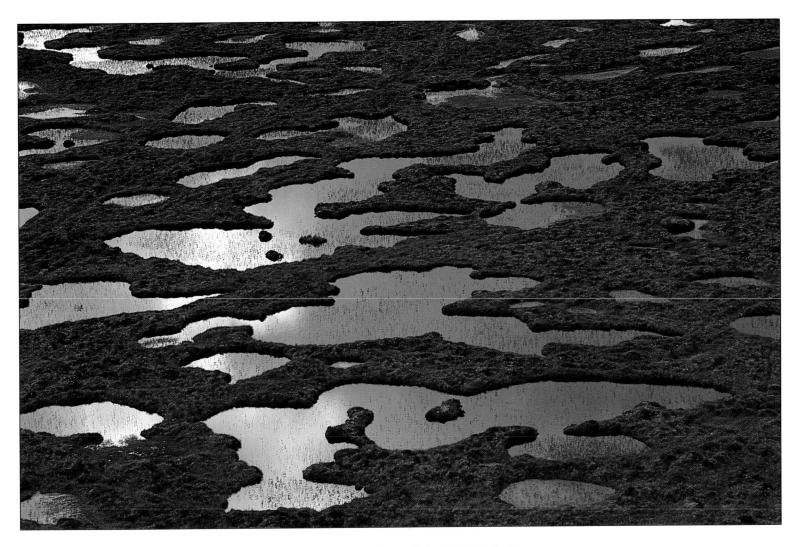

BLAR NAM FAOILEAG

Heather, cottongrass, deer sedge and bog mosses grow in this Caithness reserve.
Considered to be one of the best examples of watershed mire in the country, it
is also an important breeding ground for moorland birds.

opposite **Looking across the reserve and the flat expanse of Caithness to the mountains of the far north west**

INVERNAVER

Few trees grow at the north coast reserve of Invernaver. Here the harsh northerly winds blow sand onto the moor from the beach, creating an unusual habitat for plants. Mountain and maritime species grow close together in great profusion near sea level, and a few patches of birchwood on the slopes facing the sea provide cover for woodcock, snipe, and badgers.

GUALIN

This vast wilderness in the far north west is dominated by the imposing shape of
Foinaven, its quartzite ridges glinting with a silvery light. Great areas of rugged,
boulder-strewn plateau are broken by the patterns of loch and peat-bog, where a
variety of marsh and mountain plants are found.

NIGG AND UDALE BAYS

The inter-tidal mudflats of the Cromarty Firth in Easter Ross form an important habitat for wintering and passage wildfowl. The wigeon, whooper and mute swan, and greylag geese are attracted here by the strong growth of eelgrass on which they feed, undeterred by the activities of the nearby oil-rig fabrication yard.

above **Beyond the tidal mudflats of Nigg Bay an oil-rig sits at anchor in the Cromarty Firth**

LOCH SUNART WOODLANDS

The woodlands at Loch Sunart, a west coast sea-loch, are of two contrasting types. Ariundle Wood,
on the Ardnamurchan side of the loch, is an oakwood, with birch, hazel and rowan also present;
while the larger Glencripesdale Wood on the steep southern slopes consists mainly of ash, with some
birch, hazel and alder. Mosses and lichens flourish here in the high humidity of the western seaboard.

STRATHFARRAR

Strathfarrar is a rugged tree-lined valley which drains eastwards into the river Beauly west of Inverness. The birchwoods beneath the rocky summits contain fragments of the Caledonian pine forest, and a pinewood regeneration programme is now being carried out here. Many delicate flowers, including lesser celandine and wood anemone, grow among the birches.

INVERPOLLY

The towering sandstone peaks of Cul Mor, Cul Beag, and Stac Polly encircle the southern end of remote Loch Sionascaig in the north west. Here Inverpolly reserve stretches westwards to the sea at Enard Bay, its mountains, lochs, forests, rolling moorland and marine islands combining to form a rich variety of habitats in a vast and dramatic landscape. In terms of size Inverpolly is second only to the Cairngorms. Knockan Cliff, added to the reserve in 1962, is recognised as an important geological site. It was here that geologists in the late nineteenth century first suggested that the enormous forces in the earth's core could drive huge segments of highly altered rock over more recently formed rock – a process by which some mountain chains are formed. Inverpolly is noted for its bird life, with over a hundred species recorded, including greenshank and black-throated diver which breed on the lower moorlands and their lochs.

above Boat Bay and Loch Sionascaig, with Cul Mor, Cul Beag and Stac Polly *opposite* Stac Polly's imposing shape as seen from the north west

32 *above* Stac Polly from the peak of Suilven

GLEN ROY

The 'Parallel Roads' of Glen Roy are an important feature of Britain's geological heritage. Distinct horizontal lines along the hillsides of Glen Roy and some adjacent glens mark the successive shorelines of lakes dammed by barriers of ice at the very end of the last Ice Age. According to Gaelic folklore these 'roads' were built by mythical heroes to improve their prospects in the hunt.

STRATHY BOG

This small isolated reserve, within the wider peatlands of Caithness and
Sutherland which are at present under threat from forestry, is one of
Britain's best remaining examples of blanket bog. Dwarf birch, sundews,
and many other bog plants flourish here.

BEINN EIGHE

In 1951 Beinn Eighe was declared Britain's first National Nature Reserve. It is typical of a number of northern deer forests, with lochside, natural woodland, plantations of native pine, mountain, moor and stream. The natural pinewood along the southern shore of Loch Maree, known as Glas Leitire – 'the wood on the grey slope', is a remnant of the Caledonian Forest. Throughout the reserve a rich variety of wildlife can be seen amid some of the most striking scenery in the north west.

LOCH DRUIDIBEG

The terrain on this reserve in the Western Isles consists of moorland, croftland, machair and seashore. Loch Druidibeg on South Uist has a large colony of greylag geese and its shallow waters and fern-fringed islands support several other breeding birds, including red-breasted merganser, mute swan and heron. Hen harrier and short-eared owl also nest nearby. Further west, the croftlands, machair, lochs and shore are even richer in bird life. Here Arctic tern, ringed plover, corncrake and several species of duck and wader are found. But perhaps the most striking feature of the reserve is the machair, a unique sandy plain which divides the coastal dunes from the moorland. In summer the whole area, the largest of its type in Britain, is carpeted with wild flowers in bloom.

above **The crofting township of Stilligarry lies between Loch Druidibeg and the sea**

This sandy beach on the west coast of South Uist forms part of the reserve

next page Loch Druidibeg at dusk, the distant island of Boreray, St Kilda, is visible on the horizon

CORRIESHALLOCH GORGE

South of Ullapool the wooded ravine of the Corrieshalloch Gorge, carved out by the
river Droma, is an impressive sight. A suspension bridge gives a clear view of the Falls
of Measach as they plunge 36 metres into the canyon, while, on either side, mosses
and other plants cling to the sheer rock face.

INCHNADAMPH

The botanically rich moorland plateau of Inchnadamph lies between Loch Assynt and Ben More Assynt in Sutherland. The area is also of geological interest, with limestone outcrops, underground streams and caves. Late Stone Age relics of human occupation have been found in the caves, along with bones of bear, lynx, and arctic fox.

LOCH MAREE ISLANDS

Loch Maree, one of Scotland's best known and loveliest lochs, is thought to be named after
the Irish saint who founded the seventh century monastery at Applecross. According to
legend he lived for a time as a hermit on one of the islands. Of the forty or so islands the
largest, Eilean Subhainn, and others nearby are covered with native Scots pine and juniper,
forming a unique group of wooded islands in the north west.

RHUM

The island of Rhum lies in the Inner Hebrides to the south of Skye. Archaeological excavations of a Mesolithic camp-site have provided evidence here of some of Scotland's earliest known inhabitants. A more contemporary feature is Kinloch Castle, built in 1901 and now run as a hotel and hostel by the Nature Conservancy Council who acquired Rhum in 1957. Nowadays red deer, feral goats, golden eagles, and colonies of cliff-dwelling seabirds populate the island. The vegetation on the cliffs and mountain summits has hardly been disturbed since the last Ice Age and many dwarf shrubs and colourful cushion alpines are found here. The mountains are volcanic in origin and the name of the highest, Askival, suggests that Rhum was known to the Norsemen as a significant landmark. The high slopes of the mountains are peppered with the nesting burrows of the island's vast colony of Manx shearwaters. Rhum is an important centre for many kinds of research: geologists study its varied rock-types, controlled studies of red deer are carried out, and experiments are conducted on the restoration of woodlands. The recent successful reintroduction of the white-tailed sea eagle is yet another significant achievement.

above Hallival shrouded in cloud   *opposite* The Mausoleum at Harris with Ruinsival partially hidden by sea mist

50 *right* Looking across the island from Meall Breac

52 *above left* Askival, Rhum's highest mountain, was named by the Norsemen *above right* Kinloch Glen in April

THE SOUTH WEST

Loch Lomond, lying as it does on the Highland Boundary Fault, occupies a strategic position. To the north of its wooded banks and islands the landscape is dominated by the southern Grampian peaks of Ben Lomond, Ben More and Ben Vorlich, while to the south the softer contours of the Lowlands stretch away across Strathclyde towards Dumfries and Galloway. The more northerly reserves in Argyll, such as those at Glen Nant and Taynish, are noted for their native deciduous woodlands, like those at Loch Lomond, which have survived largely thanks to man's careful management in the past. Their rich growths of lichens and mosses are of particular botanical interest. Further south, reserves such as the Clyde Valley Woodlands and Braehead Moss represent the small proportion of land which has not been substantially altered by industry or agriculture. However, the coastal strips, marshes and granite uplands of Dumfries and Galloway go some way to restoring the balance. In this area Kirkconnell Flow, a raised mire, and Caerlaverock, famous for wintering wildfowl, are fine, contrasting examples of Scotland's natural heritage.

opposite Mosses and lichens thrive in the mild damp climate at Glen Nant on the Argyll coast

LOCH LOMOND

Britain's largest stretch of inland water sits at the heart of Scotland's most popular scenic area. The Trossachs and Loch Lomond are indeed legendary, but these wooded shores and islands are also important for nature conservation. Inchcailloch, which contains the foundations of a thirteenth century church and ancient burial ground, is the largest of five islands on the reserve. It has several different types of soil and a correspondingly rich variety of plants and trees. These mixed woodlands on the islands and lochside are predominantly oak and attract many species of woodland birds and insects. Around the mouth of the river Endrick the marshes and lagoons form breeding grounds for wildfowl, and within the loch itself many different types of fish are found, including the powan or 'freshwater herring'.

58 *above* Oak trees on Inchcailloch island

CLYDE VALLEY WOODLANDS

These beautiful, mixed broadleaf woodlands near Lanark contain a great diversity of trees and plants. Among the elm, oak, ash and alders of Cleghorn Glen a number of uncommon plants thrive, including wood fescue and stone bramble.

BRAEHEAD MOSS

This reserve, near the village of Braehead in southern Strathclyde, was purchased by the Nature Conservancy Council in 1980. It lies over 270 metres above sea level and is a typical, relatively undisturbed, example of a peat-bog. Several uncommon types of bog moss grow here.

KIRKCONNELL FLOW

This is the only reasonably intact raised peat moss on the northern side of the Solway
Firth. Peat cutting and land reclamation have reduced its size, and these activities probably
caused a slight lowering of the water level in the centre of the mire. This allowed Scots
pine and birch to colonise the area some time ago.

TAYNISH

Taynish reserve, bounded by Loch Sween in Argyll, lies on the narrow promontory where the cattle herds from Islay and Jura were once landed on the mainland. Its oak trees form one of the most important remnants of native deciduous woods in Scotland. Areas of peat-bog, grassland and heather provide rich wildlife habitats, and the adjacent shallow waters abound in marine life.

CAERLAVEROCK

Caerlaverock National Nature Reserve, which stretches along the Solway Firth south of Dumfries, is a merse or saltmarsh. It is composed of plants which can survive flooding by the sea and these provide grazing for cattle and migrating geese. Autumn sees the merse crowded with ducks and waders, and in late winter the geese arrive, including great skeins of barnacle geese from Spitzbergen. This reserve is also the most northerly breeding ground for the rare natterjack toad, a protected species.

above Barnacle geese flight over the Nith estuary   *opposite* Looking across the merse and Solway Firth to the mountains of Cumbria

66 *right* Flocks of gulls over the mudflats at low tide

THE SOUTH EAST

Much of the land in south eastern Scotland is in agricultural use. This is particularly true of the Borders, Lothian and Fife, but Tayside, bisected diagonally by the Highland Boundary Fault, still contains large, relatively undisturbed areas. In the west, Rannoch Moor, a vast exposed tract of moor and marshland, and Ben Lawers, one of several calcium-rich mountains renowned for their arctic-alpine flora, are both reserves of considerable scale and importance. The lowlands and coastal plains to the south and east of the faultline also contain significant, if less dramatic, conservation areas. The secluded waters of Morton Lochs in Fife provide a contrast with a coastal reserve such as St. Abb's Head, well-known for its cliff scenery and large numbers of nesting seabirds; while Loch Leven, midway between the Firths of Tay and Forth, is the most important freshwater area in Britain for migratory and breeding wildfowl.

BEN LAWERS

The lime-rich Breadalbane mountains in western Tayside are of great botanical interest. Of these Ben Lawers, towering over Loch Tay, is the finest example. Its scree slopes, cliff ledges and grassy corries contain a great variety of mountain-dwelling plants, among them rare alpines such as the snow gentian and alpine forget-me-not. These are found mainly in places beyond the reach of grazing sheep and deer.

TENTSMUIR POINT

Tentsmuir, at the north eastern tip of Fife, is an important roosting and feeding ground for waders and wildfowl, with large gatherings of migratory eider duck in autumn. Behind the Abertay Sands, where seals can often be seen, the dunes are gradually creeping towards the sea, demonstrating the different stages of plant colonisation. The area is also noted for its wildflowers and insects.

above **A solitary oystercatcher feeding on the foreshore**

LOCH LEVEN

This great freshwater loch near Kinross has long been renowned for its brown trout fishing. Its international status as a conservation area is due to the range and numbers of wildfowl its supports, a population which includes the highest density of breeding tufted ducks and mallard in Britain. Other wildfowl, particularly greylag and pinkfooted geese, arrive in winter to roost on the loch and feed on the surrounding land.

ST ABB'S HEAD

St Abb's Head, a rugged coastal promontory near Eyemouth, is well known for its nesting and migrating seabirds. In summer the steep lava cliffs are packed with guillemot, razorbill, fulmar and many other species; while in the autumn, migrants such as sooty and Manx shearwaters pass close to the headlands. At this time too, smaller migrant rarities such as the red-breasted flycatcher are sometimes blown ashore.

MORTON LOCHS

These man-made lochs, surrounded by marsh and woodland, were originally created for rearing trout. For many years they attracted large numbers of wildfowl and waders but by the 1960's they had become silted up. A major restoration was begun in 1976, with much of the silt being removed and used to create islands and reshape the lochs. Grass, sedges and trees were planted and now provide food and nesting cover for the many waders and migrant wildfowl which have returned to this east Fife reserve.

RANNOCH MOOR

The wild and desolate expanse of Rannoch Moor lies to the east of Glen Coe. Created by glacial action, it consists mainly of peat filled hollows, areas of mire and numerous lochs and lochans. In places where the peat has become eroded the buried remains of Scots pines are revealed, reminders of the forest which partly covered the area in earlier times. The reserve, which occupies the north east corner of the Moor, is mainly of interest to botanists but insect and bird life are also plentiful.

THE NORTH EAST

Grampian Region, where most of the north eastern mainland reserves lie, is an area of contrasts. The pine-forested valley of the Dee or the stark, brooding heights of the Cairngorms differ enormously from the flat agricultural lowlands of the Buchan plain to the east. Again, the fertile Moray coast bears little resemblance to the rugged windswept coastline south of Aberdeen. The reserves at Sands of Forvie and St Cyrus both have well-preserved dune systems and estuaries which support large populations of birds and invertebrates, while the Cairngorms and Creag Meagaidh, covering between them almost thirty thousand hectares of land, are splendid examples of mountain habitats. Muir of Dinnet, on the middle reaches of the Dee, combines some of the characteristics of both these extremes; wildfowl breed in the marshes around the lochs and a variety of upland mammals are found in the birch and pine woods. In the far north the Shetland Isles also have important nature conservation areas. Despite major oil developments these islands continue to provide a safe haven for many species of seabird, most notably on Noss and at Hermaness on Unst.

opposite A colourful pattern of lichens growing on a rock at Muir of Dinnet

CAIRNGORMS

The Cairngorms were originally known as Monadh Ruadh, the Red Mountains, because of the presence of pink felspar in the granite. It is difficult to overestimate the importance of this dramatic region of mountain, moor, loch and forest which dominates the central Grampians between the Spey and Dee valleys. It is Britain's largest reserve and it stands as a living source of information about the pre-history of our islands. Even in summer the conditions on the high plateau are sub-arctic, similar to those which covered most of northern Europe towards the end of the last Ice Age, and only the hardiest plants and animals survive here. These are the haunts of ptarmigan, dotterel, snow bunting, golden eagle and mountain hare. But in the high corries, the lower moorland and pinewoods, which include remnants of the ancient Caledonian Forest, there is a wide range of plant and wildlife. Here mountain rock cress and alpine speedwell replace the mosses and lichens of the summits, red deer roam over the higher ground, and in the woods capercaillie, roe deer and the occasional wild cat are seen.

opposite Autumn birches and a remnant of the Caledonian Forest clothe the lower slopes of the Cairngorms

84 *right* Devil's Point and the Lairig Ghru in winter

above Loch an Eilein, Rothiemurchus *opposite* Glen Einich from the air

Ben Macdui in the distance, with Carn Etchachan and Pinnacle Gully in the foreground (right). Ben Macdui, which rises to over 1300 metres, is the highest mountain in the Cairngorms range. The views here are breathtaking but the weather on the high summits is truly sub-arctic and can deteriorate very rapidly. The edges of the plateau often end abruptly in the vertical cliffs of corries scoured by glacial action.

CRAIGELLACHIE

The sheer cliffs which form part of the Craigellachie reserve overlook Aviemore. The surrounding open birchwood, one of the largest in Speyside, is rich in bird life and in summer the trees are filled with the songs of mistle thrush, willow warbler, tree pipit and long-tailed tit. Insect life is also profuse here, with large numbers of moths, including several local varieties.

ABERNETHY FOREST

The pinewoods of Speyside, of which Abernethy Forest is a fine example, are among the most extensive native woodlands in Britain. Here the pines, of varying age, height and form, grow among a mosaic of juniper, birch and open heathland. Forest-dwellers such as red squirrel, crested tit and crossbill can be found here.

SANDS OF FORVIE AND YTHAN ESTUARY

This is one of the least disturbed large sand dune systems in Britain, noted for both its unspoilt beauty and great wealth of wildlife. The reserve, which lies north of Aberdeen near the village of Newburgh, is an important centre for research and has the densest breeding concentration of eider duck in Britain. Terns also nest in the dunes and many flowering plants grow among the dune-heath vegetation. In autumn and winter the mudflats of the Ythan Estuary are thronged with wildfowl and waders.

CREAG MEAGAIDH

The central Highland reserve of Creag Meagaidh, stretching north from the shores of Loch Laggan and rising to a height of 1100 metres, is a magnificent blend of mountain, moorland and birchwood. The outstanding views from the high ground, to Ben Nevis in the west and the Cairngorms in the east, make this a popular area for hill walking. Creag Meagaidh was purchased by the Nature Conservancy Council in 1985 to save it from the threat of afforestation with conifers, and to preserve and extend its upland birchwoods. Golden eagles circle the mountain tops and red deer graze the lower slopes, while, far below, ospreys fish in Loch Laggan.

above **Looking across the top of Glen Spean at the panorama of the Creag Meagaidh reserve**

right Creag Meagaidh ensures the conservation of
natural birchwoods, such as this one at Allt Coire Ardair

MUIR OF DINNET

This reserve, declared to commemorate Her Majesty the Queen's Silver Jubilee in 1977, is located near Aboyne in Deeside. There are several different habitats here, with both birch and pine woods, and heathland and marsh around lochs Kinord and Davan. The quiet shallow waters of the lochs, with their large reed beds and surrounding tree cover, provide feeding grounds for otter and wildfowl.

ST CYRUS

St Cyrus, a small east coast reserve, consists of a long sandy beach backed by a narrow strip of dunes and low cliffs. Rows of stake nets along the shore show that the traditional methods of netting salmon are still practised here. Many species of plants and a diverse insect population live on the dune pastures and cliffs, and little tern sometimes breed on the reserve, which also attracts winter migrants.

NOSS

The small Shetland island of Noss derives its name from the Old Norse word meaning 'a point of rock'. Its massive sandstone cliffs rise vertically from the sea to a height of almost 200 metres. Great and arctic skuas nest throughout the rough moorland on the island, while the cliff ledges are crowded with the thousands of nesting seabirds which make Noss one of Europe's largest seabird colonies.

above Noss as it appears from the Shetland mainland, about eighty thousand seabirds nest here

HERMANESS

Hermaness, on the Shetland island of Unst, is a rough moorland peninsula bounded by sea-cliffs and skerries. It supports many birds, including puffin, gannet, great and arctic skua, and red-throated diver. Several species of plants flourish here at their northern extremity, and the rocky shoreline is frequented by otters and common and grey seals.

above Gannets, whose numbers here have increased to over six thousand pairs, congregate on a stack

104 Looking across the reserve in September, the moorlands support colonies of great and arctic skua

above Hermaness Hill seen from the air   *next page* Muckle Flugga Lighthouse, the most northerly point of the British Isles

THE NATURE CONSERVANCY COUNCIL

The Nature Conservancy Council is the government body which promotes nature conservation in Great Britain. It gives advice on nature conservation to government and all those whose activities affect our wildlife and wild places. It also selects, establishes and manages a series of National Nature Reserves. This work is based on detailed ecological research and survey. The headquarters for Scotland are at 12 Hope Terrace, Edinburgh EH9 2AS.

National Nature Reserves are a series of sites of national importance for study and research into nature conservation. Some are the best available examples of different types of wildlife habitats, some contain unusual communities of wild plants and animals, and yet others include natural features such as rock exposures, gorges and landslips. In Scotland there are at present 68 NNRs covering around 112,000 ha. Of this area a little over 28% is owned by the Council while about 70% is managed under Nature Reserve Agreements with owners and occupiers. The remaining area is leased by the Council.

Visitors are generally welcomed to reserves where this is compatible with nature conservation interests and the interests of owners and occupiers. A number of reserves have open access while others have restrictions. Visitors should contact the appropriate Regional Office for information about current arrangements for access to particular reserves.

The Nature Conservancy Council wishes to acknowledge the major contribution made by the land management policies of owners and occupiers of NNRs to the safeguard of these nationally important sites.

Regional Offices

North West
Fraser Darling House, 9 Culduthel Road, Inverness IV2 4AG
Telephone: Inverness (0463) 239431

South West
The Castle, Loch Lomond Park,
Balloch, Dunbartonshire G83 8LX
Telephone: Alexandria (0389) 58511

South East
12 Hope Terrace, Edinburgh EH9 2AS
Telephone: Edinburgh (031) 447 4784

North East
Wynne-Edwards House,
17 Rubislaw Terrace, Aberdeen AB1 1XE
Telephone: Aberdeen (0224) 642863

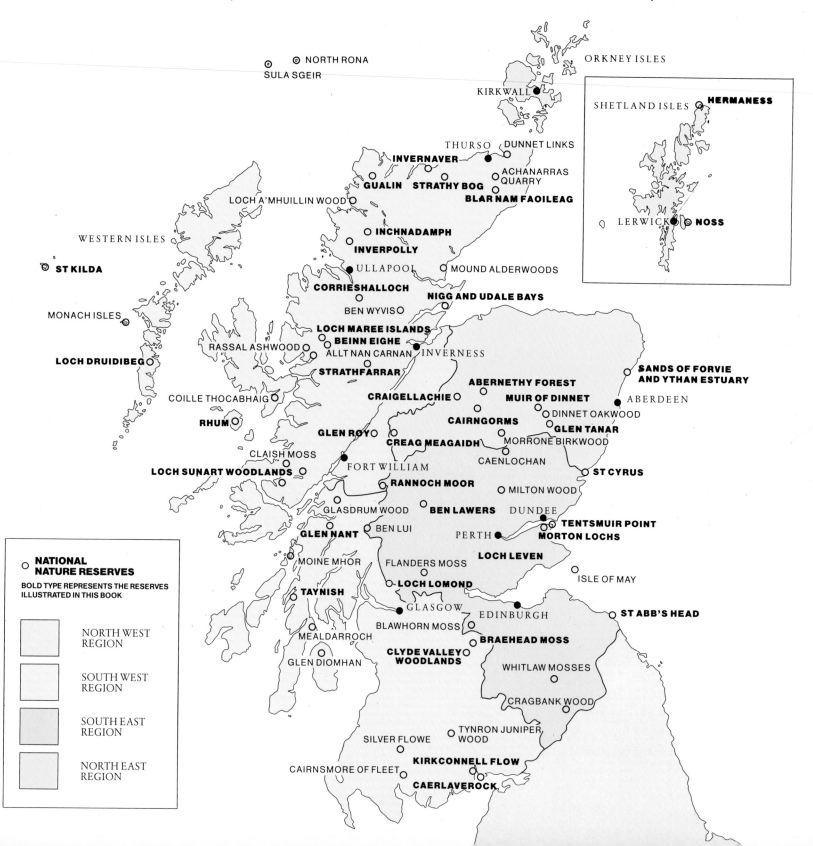

NORTH RONA
SULA SGEIR

ORKNEY ISLES

KIRKWALL

SHETLAND ISLES   HERMANESS

LERWICK   NOSS

THURSO   DUNNET LINKS
INVERNAVER
ACHANARRAS
QUARRY
GUALIN   STRATHY BOG
BLAR NAM FAOILEAG
LOCH A'MHUILLIN WOOD

WESTERN ISLES

INCHNADAMPH
INVERPOLLY
ST KILDA
ULLAPOOL   MOUND ALDERWOODS
CORRIESHALLOCH
NIGG AND UDALE BAYS
BEN WYVIS
MONACH ISLES
LOCH MAREE ISLANDS
BEINN EIGHE
RASSAL ASHWOOD
ALLT NAN CARNAN   INVERNESS
LOCH DRUIDIBEG
STRATHFARRAR
SANDS OF FORVIE
AND YTHAN ESTUARY
COILLE THOCABHAIG
ABERNETHY FOREST
CRAIGELLACHIE   MUIR OF DINNET
RHUM   ABERDEEN
DINNET OAKWOOD
GLEN ROY   CAIRNGORMS   GLEN TANAR
MORRONE BIRKWOOD
CREAG MEAGAIDH
CLAISH MOSS   CAENLOCHAN
FORT WILLIAM   ST CYRUS
LOCH SUNART WOODLANDS
RANNOCH MOOR   MILTON WOOD
GLASDRUM WOOD   BEN LAWERS   DUNDEE
GLEN NANT   BEN LUI   TENTSMUIR POINT
PERTH   MORTON LOCHS
MOINE MHOR   LOCH LEVEN
FLANDERS MOSS   ISLE OF MAY
TAYNISH   LOCH LOMOND
GLASGOW   EDINBURGH   ST ABB'S HEAD
MEALDARROCH   BLAWHORN MOSS
BRAEHEAD MOSS
GLEN DIOMHAN   CLYDE VALLEY
WOODLANDS
WHITLAW MOSSES
CRAGBANK WOOD
TYNRON JUNIPER
SILVER FLOWE   WOOD
KIRKCONNELL FLOW
CAIRNSMORE OF FLEET
CAERLAVEROCK

○ NATIONAL
NATURE RESERVES

BOLD TYPE REPRESENTS THE RESERVES
ILLUSTRATED IN THIS BOOK

NORTH WEST
REGION

SOUTH WEST
REGION

SOUTH EAST
REGION

NORTH EAST
REGION